I0878936

See Through

See Through

Frances Richard

Four Way Books
New York City

Distributed by
University Press of New England
Hanover and London

Editorial Office
Four Way Books
POB 535, Village Station
New York, NY 10014
www.fourwaybooks.com

Library of Congress Catalogue Card Number: 2002116850

ISBN 1-884800-48-3

Cover image: "Pelvis," Douglas Padgett. Graphite on paper, 2002.

This book is manufactured in the United States of America and printed on acid-free paper.

Publication of this book was made possible by a generous grant from the Greenwall Fund of The Academy of American Poets.

Four Way Books is a division of Friends of Writers, Inc., a Vermont-based not-for-profit organization. We are grateful for the assistance we receive from individual donors and private foundations.

Distributed by University Press of New England
One Court Street, Lebanon, NH 03766

ACKNOWLEDGMENTS

Gratitude to the original aesthetics interlocutors: Rob Cunningham, Mary Esther Molloy, Paul Richard, Laura Wolfe, Cory Wright. Among others. And to the writer/reader/companions: Brian Blanchfield, Caroline Crumpacker, Brenda Hillman, Nick Flynn, Hettie Jones, Miranda Mellis, G.E. Patterson, Rodney Phillips, Kristin Prevallet, Rebecca Wolff.

For material support, thanks to Martha Rhodes, who has given much more than that. Thanks to Doug Padgett and Sally Ball. Also to the Barbara Deming/Money for Women Fund, the *Marlboro Review,* Michael Carroll and the Schoolhouse Center in Provincetown, the Djerassi Resident Artists Program, and The MacDowell Colony.

Grateful acknowledgement is made to the editors of the following publications in which certain of these poems first appeared (some in different versions):

Boston Review, The Brooklyn Rail, Interim, Marlboro Review, Pierogi Press, Ploughshares, Post Road, Provincetown Arts, The Four Way Reader No. 2, UrVox.

for

DLC

RMC

MCR

Contents

The main thing is to tell a story.
It is almost
very important.

– Frank O'Hara, "Fantasy"

Always Already Hunky Dory

aureole & flicker
whispering

diadem gram mond
chronic
logue

this is how come I am drowned

~

will you stay in our lovers—
greenest pale
because it uproots the rudiments

~

but "as you were knowed as in those days"
of pre-amplitude, undivided but
I had a moiety

ooh
I would self-sabotage myself
(…to which you were going to…)

or I'd
like a flat white please, a milk
that stays fresh in a box

~

lect   gnosis

with a small piece
of chocolate

~

& ooh ooh child
"things are gonna get easier"

come back you sea, you fucking sea

the nipple
ripple

then a person wandered in and made
the landscape narrative

As if the atmosphere
of my bedroom were my one-celled
organism were the sea. As if a)

a bay window, b) blond wood pair of chairs, a table, love) my kneecaps, my
tough little china. Tea pretend

elaborate, white linoleum flecked
with gold & particles. Bathwater
greeny in the tub but genuinely there isn't depth

past texture, mottled carpet, vacant room, a
louvered door & corollary slipstream

floods the hall, embroidered moonlight made for me, a present
in material like opal. Absent *mare*

nostrum, little remedy

for dark dark and my air fern—who gave me for example
that phenomenon? Gossamer clot
of algal health, dumb lower life that sucked up

nothing quietly. That flourished—

exactly

who made whom or what where did you say. Conscious inexactitude
of ocean (in a waterglass, a bath), amoeba pathway in a smoke

upcurling from the incense burner on your dresser by your necklace
made of pink beads and your bangles and your wallet handstitched in art

therapy also. A distant metaphysic, "in the hospital." Origin of special
insecurity and here a vacant sandalwooded
room, a triple opera length with gold clasp, plastic pink

transitional object. A thee thy thou thine rope, umbilicus admired
in the mirror. Name as

sub re in de ab e pro
ject. Or whatever the hard pronoun is

for shadow. Thrown conjecture as to what

I am where how
you made
me comprehending you

—then it got very misty.

Lit signage clings to the air, corroded
vessels loose in truck flatbeds leap, clang
in the air. The street is too private.
And if in the instant of touch you acknowledge how

muscles are magnetic tape bollocksed over with everything
that ever happened to you, louvered door to the closet, a green
glassbrick place, thicker depth and a tremor of wanting

to have it two ways. Like (sudden slide drops)
underpants and a doll, pout on the threshold where nobody
answers and the original, unremastered recordings.
(Next slide drops) of beer bottle sweat, also the other

kind, acrid, a pointy
smell. Head. Crimped bottlecap, size

of a nipple, press it
into your skin for a temporary scar like a crown. (Slide) to contours
now, you can tell it is "now" by your limbs on verifiable
covers, a car horn, this robe
gaping open. (No slide. Your new issue is slippage.) So smooth
slickish petals unfurl. Uncertain relation
to metal parts, screeching

weight hurtling, crescendo
of breakage, belltone. Now comes this massive
sub-increment. Glance, a sharp

realistic thing. And you're not even sure what "alone"
means. Because

you get scared when it's bright—

Integument

Rain hangs its partition. Chlorofluorocarbon
and lamé, end of the street

by the park closed off, a silk tent.

Damask'd drapery swagged flush
frames its glass, exterior volutes grim
with pigeon-shit, rain-smell of oxygen
releasing
                    and a pressure, as of minnows
nibbling, exigence, zero, the

perfect skin on every body,
thing. An emptying, columns bruising through
the wet newspaper, gooseflesh, subtle quilting
rises, dank down coat. Sludgy minutes
quicken, air heroically
breastplate, late April, fish-scale—

Slurry in the gutter. China cabinet
and garden-apartment doors, eggshell
ceiling while the armchair's velveteen smoothes
back, back, with a fingernail, talk about
my mother, pause, *my mother*. Kleenex

and the doves' guano dissolve. Quivering bodies
of trucks at a stoplight, high panels washed
in grit like wept mascara. There is no problem, just
                    afternoon, its severe

diaphany—

Segue to instantaneous, sequin
of sun on the lawn chair's dull silver-chrome
leg. Her feet in frayed Keds, her chest tanned to freckles, mystery dated
in pencil (but lightly), acidified flyleaf inscribed so she'll know
when she read it last—

pleasure's a dialect   the plot device blurring the characters

no one literally no one must
remember anything

                        & now
it was weedy but floral aforethought, garden and farm of *her*
mother, dulcet implement rust

Minor Treatise on A Warning from Robbe-Grillet

Stunned bird rewakes in the cold
pan. Fluttering heart
placed there by hand, hand screened

in a plaid dishtowel—

When windows face each
other the thousand grassblades
quarantined in separate yards merge—

you like the phrase *mise-en-abîme*

—and the pan is named "Bake-King," innards
greased with old burnt oils. The bird's
error is transparency, okay. But could this resolve

the stove's erotic corners, enamel
curves harmed—how—as if by hammer-blows,
black metal shown through, bone

reversed. Temporarily broken-necked, small
duped-by-vision imperceptibly
revives. "Electric" is a slowly reddening

spiral, "gas" the sudden blue mandala/tit flaring
in the mother's mother's mother's muttering
dark. You set it free by the dead stump, it hops,

hooray. Dumb energy recollects itself
into itself but *if you begin*
by believing in metaphor you will end

by believing in God

If (and loons laugh

intermittently, cryptic through reeds,
mulchy shore, and)

soles sting from slapping bare stair treads, palms glow
from slapping the wall, never dare use a
fist. Then (things wait

to tattle for making them shatter: marble slab
misaligned on the dresser-top, paint on the headboard crazing
to delicate shards and) if one of the ghosts, say la transparent

matrix (the cross-mother mother) herself, plasm
in each one and each one came
to moisten me would I
tranquilize? If (insatiate safety could come when I
called how

would it then) and cuddling
into my sheets I adore
the cold seconds, before my especial heat
fans out and warms the twin bed.

Notebook #1

Achromatic and volcanic, a breathing surface, marbled-fat/lined-paper
oceanic. Snooping in the storeroom, fumes and dust, high furnace shelf.
A corrugated carton with a string.
An utter opus, vinculum. *The time before me is–*
sponges, epsom weirding here, a letter, a scrawled stoppage.

Because, as it appears, through several echelons above my head.
Looking for: whatever *it* is. Know when I find it. Like:
soft holes in it, spinal, something tangible. Excitement but not constant, not that puissant. Hush hush. Is it
inborn or extrinsic, what/how is it. Holding in my hands.
A trouble proof. A skimming, hunger for, witness material.
Made vague, turned, bleached, enveloped, invaginated.

With vacancy, Correct-o-Ribbon, Craypas, torn, secreted.
A mud/sand geological, glued suture, sliding pile, a signature.
Hasn't crumpled or scorched through though page's pH
fails and stains like linen, rusty smirch/tattoo of the flattened spiral.
Handwriting smudge and sparkle of a thick no. 2 pencil.
(blankety) (blank) illegible, birth as per your journal.
"An Experience—"

Stuck in reverie +
some disgrace at the dining room table, Wisconsin Avenue
leafy trees hectic in pattycake
clap. Air winning, always. Wouldn't you like to go
straight out the window like that—
Drifting, hating. Squat cup with its animal garland, fat
nastiness, ditty: I quit
not intentionally strangely but quit
drinking milk, tasted of green stink, bad
muck. Tablecloth swirling its spill. Against
density, psychedelic snow pattern melting as incense
would alter from thingness to smoke. Waiting for briskness, a tsking
to take it away and the table to stabilize, looking-glass glide shut
before I slide through—

tra la

Had forgotten the difference between
what is value, or hue. White noise
turned slowly to black noise and I could not
stop it, the figure had taken
a pencil or crayon and had furiously
scribbled and scribbled its outline
to mess. Empty mass, and a colorless
sidereal problem recurred. *Exeunt*
omnes, and no one and nothing
parted

Then the pointy corona of terms
slightly peeled from their sources, fiery
spikes of the static-electric
act poking into the gap

oil-swirled sloshing of brackish
rush, fresh, tidal into the gap

Slap at the hewn block the harbor
engineers had put there

to master it

the word be a verb

and I muttered it, set out extempore but land tricked me, devoured

itself, and the spiral
was gyring, styrofoam
rusted piss-yellow by salt

I was looking for that constellated

place, matter of organs reorganized, uninhabited and blackly white
nor fought in the warm rain
nor knee deep in the salt marsh

the gyring

that was my body, in English

we do not have enough
words for body

"Loverbaby" was a childhood
endearment

yes/no in the extant
inclination, still my

longing will: erode
haptic specifics, your body a strong surrogate
for dazzle, manageable portion, sippy cup
to practice my

immurement in the minute, taste, rub, whisper, *come*
into constellation like a flash of lightning

You always holding I in
pectoral astonishment, warm zone of—something

tall, a sinew undertone. Hear the speakers
singing reassuringly, basso in the viscera (...*tra*...*la*...) the organs
know

Creep back through absorption, look
galvanic: hero

pillow, pacifying mouthful
of a tacit Similac, companion where the borders breach and wash

Plus Appetite

How to be =
being. Perceive

us, A&P parking lot in determinate
dusk, grandiose

hazes fill up the sky.
Are the sky.

Shiny, cheerful aisles of plethora. So encouraging,
talkative, like a small town, overlit mutter
of—two shapes: choice
or square, two durations: a year
to a day, these substances: flesh, sheened
cardboard. Appetite

as a function
appears dumb,

cartons eager and
unctuous, idiot

surface gladhanding.
Money as dumb.

And transacting entry or exit, gracious hiss
of the sliding back, chilly
exhibit, nature. We in the ice-case
reflector, caught, given
back surplus +
influx, ugly crustacea or jetsam and flotsam, old
Vladimir, young Estragon. Sea-wrack or hunger and

aspirin. Push
at our tissue, circadian

flaring of hothouse and peatmoss on sale
in the mall portico. Cough-syrups carny

the liquor store. So we
touch. We

are touching. Ellipsis of temporary sugar
crust feeds at our mouths, hot

expiry, chrome baskets fulsome
in floodlight. Cornucopic

mess in their stanchions and car engines
billowing vapor, emitting

a cloud that is separate and mingles
with ours and fades. Toxic particulate heightens

the colors that augment or gaudily
bleed, and waves exchange
stress with the traffic, low
constant muffling roar—wait, merge—constant
comforting low muffled roar.

Dictionary Episode

I looked you up in the shallow water dictionary. It said
black and blue, said
        awkward scar, forget-me-not

noli me tangere
        kind of thing.

Foam slaps the oar-locks. Spume drowns. A stained safety
orange, salt-stiffened gloves for example, or starting
the car with a screwdriver fixed in ignition. That can be yours; I'll

        use episode, as
when the girl enters the fête in her novel, in muslin, her premodern
shift. Match-head flame in the orchid, core roseate

        with big voltage. Urge—further it. We feel shy,
as if breathless were cozy. Now this alcohol
sting of the mind, I can't read, as on marshland the windows

        are oozing, not solid but slow-moving
gel. Did you know glass is permanent liquid? So stand here
a temblor, see outer: quilts, pots, dust, excitement. And inner:

snow. It
        depends. Parts bulbed and fructified, furred
bow in rattling orchestra.
        A soughing thing fattened

and bullied by boring wind. Want that, want laugh and
        tough match-head
burns in the orchard, stripped edges. Soothe, you flare.

Corpus Orange

> we should say a feeling of *and*, a feeling of *if*, a feeling of *but*, and a feeling of *by*
>
> – William James

Orange
rhymes with nothing, try "osage"

and precious glass house, the orangerie, dearie. Replete
exotica of indoor/outdoor form. How approach, control, possession feed

the falseness of availability, climate
innocently wrong and pale with frost. Because the queen wants to be

queen of all her feeling, prepositional conjunctive

itch to be appassionata, relational, embraced. Growth in a
protected place where globey jewel appertains to tongue, the genus will

expand contract expend contact

blue lumps of lungs, blue spheroid ache you swear is true. The member
whole consists of "shiny ovate leaves and hard bright wood."

The spectral opposite of me is you.

Aporia

Craving the cookery sweets, the hot weather
ice/flour dainties.
A chipped grandma plate.
A real lady.

How a luster
simulacra—no, simile—
refrigeration. You sticky
face looking

for substance, chill & bright answer
from stasis. Untethered rock on the mantel, the
quartz vein ripped open, a
torso. Insomniac banging

her shin and floral percale not
trustworthy, sinking under
the slathering, sloughed skin, secretive,
a fainting.

Lemon, sharp bevel,
a panic of modification.
Instinctive nice
slimming of basis.

Oh don't you—
scream til you're hoarse, roughhouse
all over the landscape.
Don't you love a thousand-piece puzzle.

Yes.   Yes.

As fireworks go over the graveyard.
Spray OFF on, stomp away mad
through the gloaming. Fistful
of butterfat, napkin to sop up the dripping.

Not equivalence. Approximation.

(Her)
osteoporotic adamant, loose
sleeves of skin. Translucent meat
in sweaters, corduroy.
Compels herself as gnarl
involutes a fallen stick

rattle
(or)
grace.

An afternoon expands the whole ménage.
Blotted day, an anorectic
sky like old washed plastic. Folds
a slice of cold store bread, eats
standing, watching finches
pick.

(or)
insomnia, impalpable
gray net. Skull
faintly levitates.

(or)
That's just because I'm so mean when someone
praises health.

(or)
base paradigm of fall, the shriveling
and shucking off, the coil cracking
wide

and
(or)
renege.

Offer black coffee, contemplate
the yard. High canopy relinquishes
its sheen of chlorophyll, old-bruise yellow slowly
reappears. *It's possible*, I tell her,
to love someone and still be angry with them.
It is NOT *possible,* she says. *I don't think so.*

Heirloom basic
basin: bruised enamel, *mons Veneris*

overturned and grassblade sticking to its sweating
flank. The sopped handwashing, great and grand

the relative inheritance, rustling private
items impregnated with *durée*.

~

Mouse-shit scattered: buds of lavender between
our clean dishtowels, shade beneath the lawn chair cool and chthonic
to the ants. Frilly, chest-high, planted in sandy
soil: her asparagus bed

extends. A dainty luncheon, linen napkin, step off
from the kitchen porch, dew soaking ornament onto
her shoes. Chronic shared capacity to act

the hired girl, *the little mother of the poor*. The fondle-able bits
left over: crescent worn
into the paring blade, ubiquitous star-patterned colander.

~

Alpha and Omega
Thou art the Limit

"Now isn't that the pink-tailed limit…!"

"You may *not*…" (who saw her
crying once)

~

The cedar chest contains: a bedpan & a death mask
cast in plaster, very lovely and I kid you
not. Shirred-satin lining, suitcase filled with photos
in a panoply of brown/charcoal & ivory. Verso written on in ink, a baby
naked in the sink, a table painted paisley. Silver backing leaching lichenlike
off matching dresser mirror to show the wall.

The DNA that replicates, the bones

have such designs—

~

Fern volunteers, festoons the woods & grasps the pasture fence.
The shade beneath. A sap-white lace-trimmed
slip conceals the nacre glow of thigh, cockeyed in leaf-rot, tough
perennial. Mosquitoes perishing

in kerosene poured out to kill, each spring their larvae suffocate
and drown. She bends, so we

imagine. To prepare
the stalks to feed us she

cuts, cuts.

Postpartum (after
departure) (anywhere) depression

where a stone spun, wore itself a hole
over (time), the tongue

in groove, the hand in glove, monotony of frantic sea that keeps
on pushing the same stone on the same stone.

The pissed-off look in photos. The evaporating
kiss good-bye, your oocyte and lost love-note, your brooding.

Gleaming ontological
circumstance called "mental hospital." Called lover

in the airport, broken up (time), called repeatedly but hung up
or got only

                    the machine—

Story About *Yes*

I sat in the offices looked at the clipboard it has a blah lustrous
flange. Nubbed
upholstery. Ventilator heating
or coolant sound. I said preamble

then just that you killed
                                        (killed, you committed

                    sui generis

yourself) blank. Yuck. Nod. All the tenses and.

Distance of carpeted floor.

Exhale, then in brisk tones fast
forwarding, jotting, not looking at me, *Did you find her?*

No, space. Transparent
wrong, stupid never. Unreportable vanisher
leaving for work, a raincoat. I can vouch
for morning preschool and what passes
for world reassembles its subsequent whirring
heaves all afternoon you   fall
                                          change, I
play blocks, eat graham crackers,
drink juice. Blur. Unclear. Zilch

kept, all x-ed, something opened

the body of normal

and splashed in obliterate
                                        no—

But frail tickle in muscle, dark
ponytail, taste of hot plush. Pulse, gargantuan
shapeshift, upwelling, not out loud,
near. Explain

that I thought and the office
dilated, feral
happiness rose in my throat. Before I remembered
the question I almost said
yes—

Frequency

Piano strikes A and every A
in the house has to vibrate. Sentence ends in

emphasis, a long thrum

bidirectional, belief in A for A's sake. Along a tendon
twanged by language (a long time ago, an age)
perhaps about "the mirror stage" when picture disattaches,
leaps from murk. Vaporous day

beginning oscillating, incomplete, incompetent.
So pianissimo. And lumpen hoping

ooh... To quote quote

SEE

the lullaby, the woken-up-from stealthy
knowledge dyed by fumaroles of sunset (-rise)
imbrued on skinlike/scrimlike, interstellar, exobiological
a void. That radio

(to no one, then, is whom
she spoke? the house so sleeping, cigarette-tip silent
chord of umbra on the air) (her sitting
there—the tumblers clicking in the lock, the tumbrel
chair—alone, her coat on maybe?) (as I crept
in bare feet down the hall to)

quote quote see.

"In real life"

imprint of the basic instrument, a longing for the way

a mirror in a photo is refusenik, pure synecdoche,
raw flash. Oh alpha, ah omega, ditty about its
body while the echo keeps (the pallid floor, my
feet) (her
morose grace) repeating its
vibration from

the physical before
I woke up tingling   before
I was ever born.

Rose

> That is why we can say: "A rose is not a rose. That is why it is an authentic rose."
>
> – Thich Nhat Hanh

Let deliquesce from inside: eye
pattern of instance, sheer panel
or gristle entrail.

For awhile, then clean
til the nothing, stream outward. Run faster til
that—

As students of physics run
spastically downshore with clipboards, timing
the waves.

Thinking in chronically
limited format about

sharing, or
being shared into,

inundation so peaceful, spontaneous—that and
its pliable
shock—

As in when is a jar
not gray, not round, a mere door in the
oxygen? Firefly

lantern, the birthday-cake sparkler,
sudden happiness out in the yard.
The rose

in my dirt, shirt, or skirt,
baby
I am all

sprawled around. Disarrange
phosphorescence, at each step the ocean

kicks dazzle back. Night
flares. Cozened
out of safekeeping—

Rock
in the creak of boat-planking, slop
of rote shape, a

fresh cognizance. As in, Firefly? I'll be
your fucking firefly.

Lie again, where cold front
hits the warm, recast
surface as core. Compare *kapalabhati,*
"the skull-shining breath," or à la
rain that fell, transposed itself
to hug vacant lot objects. Sheath. Bedclothes. Glacé
and farty heat, I am your
trumpet vine, twining convolvula—

Twitch, heavy perquisite on tree limbs, power
lines, excess laminated, glabrous,
poised. The whole world as a clinking silent crystal
chandelier, the quasi
—rather, pseudo—bucolic
ailanthus drags.

Your sudden running-dog dream. Sun

not melting it—

a barrier
hums around me, cool force
field, myelinated nerve.

Morphoplasticism
of the ur-force, rumpled
bed
    room gridded
    with glimmer and paneled
    in total sub-meaning

denoting   your phrases, your

instrumentality   weft of a physics in action, in

wooziness cast by
penumbra through ricepaper wind-slapping
shade. Inchoateness as

synesthesia   as *I want! I want!*

    when marrow precipitates
    via each
    surface and face

~

Sequencing
guise + aspect, adumbrate the synaptic
info, the arcing

between   of your phases

all the musico-lyrico-chemical + satiation

fears   lead to retreat to
inanity suborned by   eeek!, by an eking

out of distinction   a grappling back
from imprinting   or being impressed

~

so would you like a cup of tea or
something so
what are you thinking now

Silver Cup Studios

Across the riverness. Reflected
on the scummed estuarine wash, upcurrent from the
DOMINO sugar dock. A *verité folle.* The present
slipping out. And so it happens

to be dusk again, predictably, because you crave
crepuscule and are
yourself unsure. People are not like landscape. Even
landscape is not.

Grain of molecule.
Murmur's sex. Encrypted

or describe such nondescript, low comforting
drone, an autoerotic ode to. *Flâneur*-ify: new hyacinth, drab awning
or soot window briefly bronzed, storey-high frowzy neon
stutters on reliably. Nice blight.

Your campfire tale. Your lovenest. All
unreals—
Unclarity: is ownership

a picture and does pleasure give confidence. The sodden mattress
bulges, silky pallet
in the weeds, read bubble-writ, enshadowed
tags spraypainted. Your name

for this, the tender lurid surface means
the river doubles as the river. Does stability—what. Something.
Does it please.

Milk Tongue

good
gibberish

vowel thumbsuck

luscious
ferocious

vague: *id est*

mm mma *ah*

~

her ample/simple
syllable (
) grunt satiety
we held

by fragrant wall, dim
rush, a rushing

~

repeat
systole and diastole

no margin *warm* *thrum* ooh
la la

~

or cite as evidentiary old
brochure for “the” La Leche League

groovy illustration
in brown ink, funky madonna
        stain

~

        it (lilts and sticks) (is sticky)

~

        disrememberment

trite likeness of the
blurred whatever core

        this dress
        couch
        year
        size   hot and small
        this fluid ostinato in the
                            protozoa core

~

insistently

vestigially absorbed &

patting
complacency

(not) comprehending
tactile
attachment, air vs. liquid wave

vanish pat

warm bone articulates
all skin a code

~

astringent, bluish

dribble rag, thin luxe

to calcify
to vaporize

~

Re: conjugate the
conjugal nice kitchen, pour

jug, clunk ceramic
from her hospital program

root project, i. e. flowers grown

in bowls, surrogate
sluice earth
                    the paperwhite narcissus

just happy on
          stones + water

                              flourish
pretty   simple
happy

~

          while on the locked-door ward
                    she sat & smoked
          orality
suck shock

~

the schizoid
                    delectation

bulbs split
                              open, stark
                              light goes out

stalk thrives. Fragrant
from nothing:

(*mmm   o the   her*
nature wins

again)

fool oxygen
fat nutrient
pure screen

On Peekaboo and the Pathetic Fallacy

—or breathing's disappearance qua
California, ether
of eucalyptus, hills like pelt
spread over muscle, bruised succulents.
Black ocean lapping, lapping, and erosion
throws itself at the freeway, giddy mud
penned in, restraining wire. Who is the cliff
that can't hold on, that slides? Contours
self-transfiguring, traffic blocked. "The only constant
is impermanence." "Get home safe!"
You and me—these precincts

bearded with seaweed—your body.
Igneous, milky. Halo flash on windshields at sunset, scary vestiges
of heaven, cop's mirrored glasses. So
we lived inside this tang. "Object constancy"
means the infant believing past the blanket, bougainvillea
uncancelled by the fog. And liquefaction, faults
and rupture: natural. But it hurt, the seized-up
lung—

Dulce night to climb
the hill spine, spoor
to follow rustling, step
through violet nada. Amniotic
cessation/push of breeze.

~

Smear of lightish
nylon, wavering
bearing of your clothes. Gauge myself
by your dissolving and so
wanting to dissolve.

~

Sandstone particles
polished off til boulders
effloresce as caves. Multifoliate
and winged quanta
adjust.

~

Voluptuous geological
silhouettes. This land is your
musk, analogue, trace
chapparal, brume, diesel,
creosote.

~

Caress.
In each interstice
of gnarl and striation, contours
of coastal night-fog
of raw come-apart.

~

As if a membrane
stretched before admitting us.
Rock broken by twin holes,
pelvic. Discs of distant
pivoting nightfall.

~

Fine grains adhere
in sweat. So kissing mimics
licking boulder curves and I
sieve—

waking, I could swear
plain moonlight caused this noise.

a kid I fell into the milk

– *Orphic Fragments*

Of comely, gluey
disappointment, caustic leak
between the slats of instant one
and instant two. My substance must approximate

a precious thing, but slightly
wrong, endearing
little patch of mediocrity, circumference
pulled close, close. Hard

math. The sparrows or whatever
commandeer a square of quiet, pock it with their audibility.
Enormous harsh vibration when the boosted-stereo vehicle
glides past. Deflowered desert, horned

panorama wrapped
arrhythmically around the tight horizon. Where
we're camped, the ripstop tent flap slaps
its radiant panels in the dawn. The hills

bend down. A vascular
contraction in each interval, your
constancy, consistency, viscosity that sticks me.

brought/awakened
taught/forsaken

(glukupikron
glukupikron)

I am stuck

Notebook #2

Old linoleum vista, hallway lesson in perspectival recession.

Skip.

Cabinet doors, couch slipcovers in summer, a kitchen, a dirty white child.

Skip.

Explorers in tundra stumbling forth in a blizzard.

Live lichen under ozone's bald opening.

Incessant re- and re-reading. Arguing, trilling.

Triumphant and violent, icecap distorting the earth's two egg-pointed ends.

Magnetic, a penguin.

A newsprint newspaper. A crossword.

Ink shadow comes off on the heel of the hand that's been pressing.

Skip.

Heroes, magicians. Plucky girls in the midst of all situations.

Paperwhite sucks up its normal tapwater to blossom.

Mind grinds morphology, dinner plate, crustal subduction.

Here is a core thesis statement.

Act natural. Box of an unguent. Skip. Dear dairy diary.

Then when the prince comes.

The queen plus the dowager. Wish versus manifestation.

Leap

        Sheet lightning
        mirror, nauseate

the deep grinning wall. Infinity

                impulse, ballet-class piano
        jangles, shreds
damp, spongy air. Shoot forward in

                                spirals, in
                vacuum, in cleft
                        overwhelm. Modal
        skip to can't-breathe
                "infinity"

I would have said that word
then. And 1-2-3
            1-2-3 spin face

away but stay
        ostracized by infinity—I said
                        "ostracized." And

repeat. Leap

between folding chairs shapeless
with jackets, shoes, bags, mothers' watching
heats fug our leaps stir in the studio and mine: sheer

        space. Pinkness blurring the vertical
mercury, lurid

D-A-N-C-E mixing
in
on
off
high
through the window—

Vacant billowing crack.
I cried and had to be taken out.
Afterwards we went to McDonalds. Alternate

ballast, gulp to dope clutching
tantrum. Not because

no one saw. But corps perfected/
invisible proves absence
has substance, it
wafts.

So as I moved, I moved
through her.

Because she was space—

Inner Color of Water in Depressions Peels Away

Pacific peels away and in depressions
where a stone spun, trapped
a lens, cupsful of loose
primordial—
Cold laps & numbs
bare feet but squat, grip slick
juts, adjust.
Where all forms

nub + encrustation, spiny, conical
distillate and/vs.
mass enormity,
you wear a flannel shirt, faint
odor, tea-tree oil. Tentatively

ecstatic, cull my trophies
that I put wet in your pocket, shield them.
Peer. Sea
cucumber, gelatinous mottled
slug, horned sensor, or the starfish wedged
in niches, private
stroke, the
burnt-orange-purplish radial symmetry

—tendon stretched, *silk*
of the thigh
smooth inner patch (I've often
thought : briny creature
handful, shy)—

Horizon wipes to shimmer, orangeish
crux, Pacific Coast Hwy

hushes. Rolling
                        hushing gray
                                    symphonic constancy
                                    arrives. To eat
its littoral. Moist, glottal form
                        mollusk
            echinoderm, bemused in squirm. By

                                    sway. Your forefinger guides
mine into anemones where cilia catch, tear blandly, hermit crabs
                        joust their blue legs. Meridian all

rhythmical, pared off. Hair blowing in coronas
                        stinging, blinding—

0°

How many more insomnias will this cost may I ask and why the
coup de foudre, why "uncomfortability" or "intimist"
for that matter loop, arrogance re: order, proper animist
geography but more so damage, matter?

How much degree of elemental are you? Liquid, mineral, not
"are you?"—sure you are—but scatterbrain futurity
wants to know who is in charge here, where here is, and
if the porous rock, the *come in under* *the shadow of this red rock*

will help? Does matter? If not, so will the kaleidoscopic, kinesthetic
work and iterate, impaired distinction grooving in a damaged
lassitude? Other dweller in a permanent vacillation zone, an
underbelly, peach or shelter magics

melt into the *sea, eventually*

I "misunderestimated," yes, but it was
good terror

A Last Great Problem in a Specialized Field

> For this equation I have discovered a marvelous proof, but the margin is too small to contain it—
>
> – Pierre de Fermat, 1637

allege a ledge.   *containment*

shellacked with pigeon shit.   *embedded diamond-wire in the window.*

pattern soldered in   *transparent strata*

pebbled, frosted, grimed   *wood sash yanked up.*

a marble margin   *inside touching outside concrete sill.*

width in inches equal to both   *feet on porcelain tile. old enamel*

paint, a ladies'   *public toilet, airshaft wind*

that whooshes back.   *fine linens, shoes, bone*

china are arrayed beyond the door.   *department store.*

mid-morning, the fourth floor.   *pinfeathers waft.*

a chasm day.

a cooing.

cleaving calculation.

poised   *and ineluctable the forcible*

can't-not-imagine goad, numb   *day job yields.*

wrong logic.

to marvelous balance.

constant gritty wind.

teeter, inspire, marrow roar and answer   *is the vanishment of*

answers, you   *great questioner.*

is four floors high   *enough. is this particular*

flash total. narrow   *uncontainable, you*

theorem.

into which

a distance merged

A Lava Lamp

Gist insinuating
          gracious crisis, keen
parenthesis. Accumulating disappearance, sound on mute
and picture Vaselined, slo-mo and gauzed.

A vacant blurb. Hearsay and qualm seep, kick and scream about
          such rupture but in an
          attenuated mode. What authorized
this cute wish for entirety any
way (a "parent
                    thesis")—

Craving to be fluent, quasi kiss. Premise garbling at
inept speed, innards shifting, ozone ooze,
a lava lamp

~

          While outspread there—a green tea
glint on actual ocean, cloud + rock. Lost through
chiasmus, "to stop too fearful and too faint
to go," while occurrences
keep meting more stuff out.
                    Renew attentiveness, jump-cut
to the hot
          oak-leaf-strewn path, a gas-blue lizard
          darts across, a skink. You think this

emblematizes—what right
byword—zeal, facticity. Though kiss elongates
          in the whistling, in the viscous elemental
                    isn't-even-there, a Muzak

crooning gimmick

(cradlesong of
x-ed out gist)

        & look: the corpse
raccoon, floating
with its back humped. Stimulus, a

(murk) (morass) (exposure) wet fur
slicked to show a (stay with it, the sorry) strip of skin, gray/pink.
        & you excited
by excitement and the paws' nude,
fetal curl, pearl
snout pointing toward bottom and all territory
sunk, this hour
slurping mother-of-inner-shell
sheen off the water.

Spectrum of petroleum (chimerical). Close (melting)
shipping lane. The fancy houses and your prowess, shoulder flexions
iterate their sotto voce *pull down strong out pull*, and if you poke it
with your paddle, it will genuflect,
resist. Glove-tip

sliding over its neat sac (of local silt)
of estuary. Each coarse hair separate, combed—

...and when I'm sad, she comes to me

from skinned-knee lattice

on the asphalt scoured in, mirage or frieze

of quell and thrill collide. She penetrates

between the heaves of storm—

she means I

couldn't love you if (   ), she means I

flare up witchy (   ), emanating

off you like a smell. Frieze of

think-you're-specialness.

Mirage of

twittering nuclei, the scald of *stillness in the air* but glee

makes banshee uplift, fierce permission, she

says run around outside in birthday suit in downpour, catalyze

this (   ). She means you

will have to (   ). But commensurate

with aftersparkle, gasoline prismatics, stay.

Take anything you want from me...

Song (Trad. Arr.)

A long & burnished
hallway, bells. Bent charge nurse in a halo
at her desk.
Rain fatiguing
snow and lightning ardent, fog,
we asked if
she saw ghosts massed, beckoning.
Her vision
locked.
I whispered
to her coma and
a garden party
assembled on the porch, orchidlike
paper lanterns and an orchestra tuning up. Her
parents' cronies dancing, nineteen ought.
That was an hour.
Fingertips gauged her chest.
Determined panting, then I reminded her
how she would try to find
an interval in the wind, she'd whisper
Look you guys.
Not a breath stirring.

That was an hour. Someone
sat. I slept. Chrome, night cries &
motors, oxygen's sibilance. A box of
distilled water moistened it.
Her panting. Inward.
Sternum mobile, resolute
pulse answering faint pressure
my hand put. Yes. I'm here. Not yet.
An hour.

An hour. Aides
brought trays and juice. Snow
sharpened, blued to gold,
                    her facebones
                                changed. A watching,
firelit. We stretched and bent. A palm
got cool on her hot forehead, an hour, hot on her cool
forehead. She wore a rakish knitted
pink beret. Someone whispered
          "Hello, Mrs. Hat."

I sang a bit. Her panting inward
                    concentration, absolute. The leisure
of their summer dress, simpatico
gathering. Drinks, laughter, chat. Look you guys.
                    The morning. Fluttering—

Discarnate

Thunderheads project an ion shadow
on the ground, I mean they urge the earth
to pull down lightning

            (textbook night) "We"—figures—

loiter in the lowlands, by the plashing
place, mosquitoes fascinated by the data
our heat pours. Lush humming
cloud, the rotten green

Wisconsin blazoning our bodies with astir.

A diagram: a rural, overlit transparence of the
frosty mug, laminate counter, as excited
in two quiets you and I both
watch the storm twitch, lightning strobing

hectically *no* rapturously *no*

it cannot leave the hill alone it vibrates trees
backlit/foreground in blackish-purple sync
with their own x-ray silhouettes—

I itch, am bitten. Stall, run off the road
with pouring froth, this is a summer night,
a paroxysm.

~

And figures bruise
            (a pileup of strato-

cumulo-yearning) scribbles
show how negatives accrue, the dirt holds

agitation and the sky
jumps. Crash, fade, charge. "We" atomized
in onslaught can't be
right. Shall I compare

your aspect to the Instamatic flashcubes
devil-eyed in childhood snapshots? A little

vista, seismic
looking back—

Humidity lies down on me, it weighs
as much as you.

~

Through hours of humid
privacy you did not
need me once. My doze
ecliptic, startle of prodigious
demiurge

(long cliché night) "We"—keening—

thunderstrike. Uptending arrows in the figure
show how condensations coalesce, as droplets
drag the light around the glass, the sluicing
creams.

New ions burn—

And having seen *no* felt *no* known
that sudden face, red phosphor focal glance, how can it
(and it can't not) dissipate. Count a second
for each mile separating flash and clap.

        Fore*gather* or
                        to pressure

        to diminishment—

As out among
the soaking volumes, equilibration
preens itself, incarnate
pyrotechnic sweats away.

Abandon

Veins fissure every drift, economy
of branches, voice
dilutes. Windbreaker lilts

open, abandon—

Tinkling quiet.

Gob of minutes
fatten, slip. Sharp
syrupy percolate, adrenaline

fermenting, fight/flight collapse
to quartz. Cessation. Nobody circles back

to rescue you, claustrophobe
paralyzed by full expanse—

With lungs balked, pocketed
fists. Orchestral

tuning-up of silence, bushes oscillating
in brief gust. Nothing else—

not counting slush, puff of exhaust
arrested where a car passed, a million
junctures—

~

Decide. To drop the interlude, the see-through
motherlode. Not-quite bonanza. Refulgence

dabbed in ditches shot by sunset and the creek
enjambs, speeds through, refreezes. Blast
        of music. Loud tune playing
in your head—

Historian of the Immediate Future

A block.

Impedimenta made of twinges, fast-
forwarding fascination of black ice, big car, brick wall.

You thought you would be famous/dead/in jail.
I thought *flat eeek*. But sleep reconstitutes & floats in

difference midst oneiric right behind (you worry/don't)
or
left behind (by you)

the two cheeks rosy, rosy. Lick—

Infinite patience brings

immediate results. A gentle slap/the other slap
awake. Thought in vaguely 2D shape: I would be not dead
but unrecognizable by now.

Other Symposia

It was near here. In a street
similarly shining, going to the movies, and when

you asked your new acquaintance, who was quoting
the *Paradiso*, "what does [sic] mean?"

    "sic transit gloria mundi for example"

            & you felt
    stupid—

Then the Callery pears, fruitless clouds
of urban bloom stood up. Other days lit, globed
by pretty evening, all the poisons
caught reflective, and now ruined petals come slanting
toward your hair.

    In the overwhelming library
you saw this sign. Someone's name, a boneless
waving hand, then

    pink tree
    pink tree
    pink tree
    pink tree

in pink ink taped haphazardly
to a swinging door. Argument ensued inside
about the nature of subjects and beyond
the door a sole magnolia
dropped a perfect petticoat of itself onto the lawn

Quoted Material

~

this is how come I am drowned: "Drowning (II)," Grace Paley. *New and Collected Poems* (Gardiner, ME: Tilbury House Publishers, 1992), p. 8.

come back you sea, you fucking sea: "The women let the tide go out," Grace Paley. *New and Collected Poems* (Gardiner, ME: Tilbury House Publishers, 1992), p. 10.

will you stay in our lovers: "Kooks," David Bowie. *Hunky Dory*, Virgin Records, 1971.

ooh ooh child, things are gonna get easier: "Ooh Child," The Five Stairsteps. *Step By Step By Step*, Buddah Records, 1970.

each one and each one: "The Blessed Virgin compared to the Air we Breathe," Gerard Manley Hopkins. *The Oxford Authors: Gerard Manley Hopkins*, ed. Catherine Phillips (Oxford: Oxford University Press, 1986), p. 159.

pleasure's a dialect: "Indy," C. S. Giscombe. Unpublished poem, used by kind permission of the author.

no one literally no one must remember anything: "Listen to Me," Gertrude Stein. *Last Operas and Plays*, ed. Carl Van Vechten (NY: Vintage Books, 1975), p. 391.

the word be a verb: "Genesis II," Etheridge Knight. *The Essential Etheridge Knight* (Pittsburgh: University of Pittsburgh Press, 1986), p. 102.

nor fought in the warm rain / nor knee deep in the salt marsh: "Gerontion," T.S. Eliot. *The Waste Land and Other Poems* (NY: Harcourt, Brace & Co., 1958), p. 19.

come into constellation like a flash of lightning: "Convolute N: On the Theory of Knowledge, Theory of Progress," Walter Benjamin. *The Arcades Project*, trans. Howard Eiland and Kevin McLaughlin (Cambridge, MA: Belknap Press, 1999), p. 462.

the time before me is: Camera Lucida, Roland Barthes. *Camera Lucida: Reflections on Photography*, trans. Richard Howard (NY: Hill & Wang, 1981), p. 65.

Alpha and Omega / Thou art the Limit, "Hymn to the Virgin," Elizabeth Bishop. *The Complete Poems 1927–1979*, (NY: The Noonday Press, 1979), p. 221.

brought / awakened...taught / forsaken: "Sweet Bitter Love," Aretha Franklin. *Sweet Bitter Love*, Sony Records, 1970.

melt into the sea, eventually: "Castles Made of Sand," Jimi Hendrix. *Axis: Bold as Love*, MCA Records, 1967.

come in under the shadow of this red rock: "The Waste Land," T.S. Eliot. *The Waste Land and Other Poems* (NY: Harcourt, Brace & Co., 1958), p. 30.

Stillness in the Air— / Between the Heaves of Storm—: No. 465, Emily Dickinson. *The Complete Poems of Emily Dickinson*, ed. Thomas H. Johnson (Boston: Little, Brown, 1960), p. 223.

and when I'm sad, she comes to me / take anything you want from me: "Little Wing," Jimi Hendrix. *Axis: Bold as Love*, MCA Records, 1967.

Notes

~

If you begin by believing in metaphor you will end by believing in God: This warning paraphrases—in the words of a lost source—a thought from Alain Robbe-Grillet. See *For A New Novel* (Grove Press, 1965. Translated by Richard Howard).

Similac is a popular brand of infant feeding formula.

Shallow Water Dictionary is, incidentally, the title of a book-length essay by landscape historian John R. Stilgoe (Princeton Architectural Press, 1994).

Kapalabhati, literally "skull-shining," is a yogic breathing technique or *pranayama* said to release impurities from and increase electrical charge in the body.

Silver Cup Studios is a film and television soundstage in Long Island City, Queens.

"Milk tongue" is a variant for "mother tongue" or native language. The La Leche League is a community service organization that educates new mothers about lactation.

The *Orphic Fragments* are a collection of Greek hymns and lyrics attributed to Orpheus, collected and transcribed in the 6th century B.C. *Glukupikron*, "sweet-bitter," is an adjective coined by Sappho to describe Eros. See Anne Carson, *Eros the Bittersweet* (Dalkey Archive, 1998).

According to Ayurvedic philosophy, orange is the "inner color" of water.

Pierre de Fermat was a 17th century mathematician whose lost theorem, mentioned in a cryptic note in the margin of his *Euclid*, remained a classic problem in mathematics until proven by British mathematician Andrew Wiles in 1995. "A Last Great Problem in a Specialized Field" was the *New York Times* headline announcing Wiles's proof.

Historian of the Immediate Future is, incidentally, the subtitle of a biography by Nigel Whiteley of architectural critic Reyner Banham (MIT Press, 2001).

Frances Richard is an educator and critic who has taught at Barnard College, New York University, and The New School for Social Research. She has been the recipient of the 1999 *Marlboro Review* Prize, chosen by Brenda Hillman, and a grant from the Barbara Deming/Money for Women Fund. She is nonfiction editor of the literary journal *Fence*, an editor of the art and culture journal *Cabinet*, and a frequent contributor to *Artforum*. She lives in Brooklyn.